"Miss Pell Would Never Misspell"

and Other Painless Tricks for Memorizing How to Spell and Use Wily Words

BRIAN P. CLEARY

Illustrated by **J. P. SANDY**

M Millbrook Press · Minneapolis

To Sister Rose Elizabeth, O.S.U., and her
young students in El Salvador
—B.P.C.

To Joyce, Eric, and Michael
—J.P.S.

Millbrook Press
A division of Lerner Publishing Group, Inc.
241 First Avenue North
Minneapolis, MN 55401 U.S.A.

Website address: www.lernerbooks.com

Main body text set in Churchward Samoa Light 12/14.
Typeface provided by The Chank Company.

Library of Congress Cataloging-in-Publication Data

Cleary, Brian P., 1959-
    "Miss Pell would never misspell" and other painless tricks for memorizing how
to spell and use wily words / by Brian P. Cleary ; Illustrated by J. P. Sandy.
        p.   cm. – (Adventures in memory)
    Includes bibliographical references and index.
    ISBN: 978-0-8225-7822-2 (lib. bdg. : alk. paper)
    1. English language—Orthography and spelling—Juvenile literature.
    2. Vocabulary—Juvenile literature. I. Sandy, J. P. II. Title.
    PE1145.2.C54 2012
    428.1—dc22   2010051522

Manufactured in the United States of America
1 - DP - 7/15/11

HOW THIS BOOK WILL HELP YOU MEMORIZE SPELLING FACTS

Mnemonic
(pronounced *nih-MAH-nik*)

is a fancy word given to little tricks or devices that help us memorize important facts. Some of them rhyme, such as,

"Columbus sailed the ocean blue in fourteen hundred ninety-two."

Other memory aids build a word made up of the first letters of a list we're trying to memorize. **HOMES** is a trick for remembering tthe names of the five great lakes (**H**uron, **O**ntario, **M**ichigan, **E**rie, and **S**uperior). The word *HOMES* contains the firt letter of the name of each lake.

Still other memory tools are more visual, meaning that a picture will help us to remember a fact, such as this one: **A Bactrian camel has a back shaped like the letter *B* turned on its side. A Dromedary camel has a back shaped like the letter *D* turned on its side.** So we know a Bactrian camel has two humps and a Dromedary camel has one.

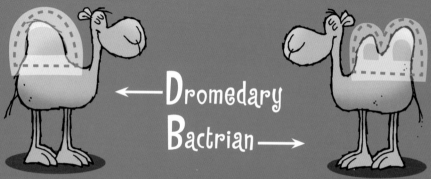

←——Dromedary
Bactrian——→

In this book, you'll find lots of fun spelling and word usage tips. But what I'm really hoping is that you'll develop your own tricks. Oftentimes the words, silly rhymes, or crazy sentences that you invent will be the most meaningful way for you to remember something!

Here's an example of what I thought of to memorize the correct number of *c*'s and *m*'s in the word ***recommend***, which I used to always have trouble spelling. I think of **1 coat and 2 mittens**, and it reminds me to use **1 *c* and 2 *m*'s**. That works for me. But if you want to remember 1 clown and 2 mud pies or 1 cat and 2 mice, it might be more meaningful (and therefore memorable) for you to do so.

Sometimes, it's the absurd nature of what you've come up with that will help you to remember. They say that **elephants never forget**. Well, now that you know about mnemonics, neither will you!

ABSENCE

This word is tricky because it has two **S** sounds—one made by an **S** and the other by a **C**. When you hear **ab_s_en_c_e**, think of an absence from _s_chool. In both words, the **S** comes first and the **C** comes second.

ARITHMETIC

To spell this word, just remember the first letter of each word in this sentence:

A Rat In Teacher's Hair Might Excite The Innocent Children.

ATTENDANCE

Not sure how to spell the ending of this word? Think: If you want to go to the **dance** Friday night, **attendance** at school is mandatory. You can also picture this sign promoting the dance. The three words in it spell attendance:

AT TEN: DANCE

BACKGROUND

Spelling this word will be easier if you remember that it's a combination of two words, **back** and **ground**—NOT back and round.

back

ground

BALLOON

Balloons are often round like a ball, so remember that the letters **b-a-l-l** begin the word **balloon**.

BECAUSE

To spell this word, remember the first letter of each word in this sentence:

Big Eels Can Always upset Small Eels.

BELIEVE

Not sure whether the *i* or the *e* comes first here? Think of the phrase "**I believe**," and put the *i* first.

CONSCIENCE

If you can spell *science*, you can spell *conscience*. Just add the letters **c-o-n** to the word **science**, and let your conscience rest.

CONTAGIOUS

The end of this word can be a little difficult, so think:

"Gee, I hope I'm not contagious."

Then you'll remember that the *g* and *i* come before the *-ous* ending.

DESSERT

This word has two **s's**—because you always want two **s**weet, **s**ugary **desserts**, not just one.

FEBRUARY

For most of the country, this is a cold month. Make the **brrr** sound as you shiver, and you won't forget the **b-r** when you're spelling this chilly word!

FRIEND

If you're not sure whether the *i* or the *e* comes first, just remember a true friend will be with you until the end, so **fri_end_** ends in **e-n-d**.

WE'LL BE
FRIENDS
TO THE END!

FINISH LINE

HEIGHT

We use numbers when we measure things such as height. Think of the number **eight**, and you'll spell **height** right!

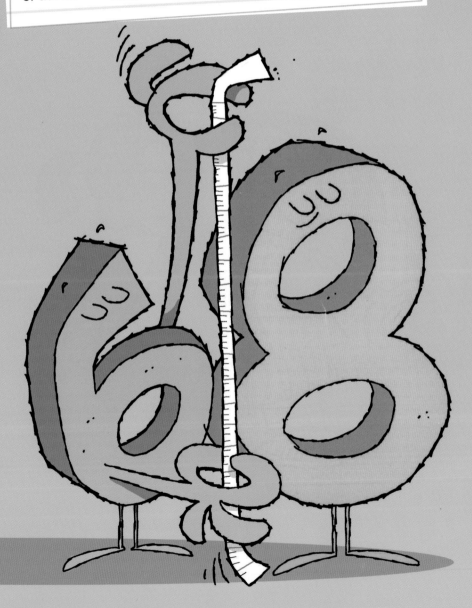

INSTRUMENT

Look for the word **_strum_** in the middle of this word. When you're playing the guitar, which is an **instrument**, you'll often strum it.

JUGGLE

You wouldn't have much fun if you tried to juggle just one thing, so put two **g**'s in the middle of this word.

LICENSE

This word is challenging because a **c** and an **s** both make the **s** sound. If you picture a li<u>ce</u>n<u>s</u>e plate made out of **licorice sticks**, you'll remember the **l-i-c** in the beginning and the **s** for sticks near the end.

MISSPELL

Aa Bb Cc Dd Ee Ff Gg

Miss Pell

Here is our teacher, Miss Pell. She would never misspell *misspell*.

NECESSARY

Not sure how many **c**'s or **s**'s are in this word? Think:

it's necessary to wear one coat and two shoes.

That's one **c** and two **s**'s.

NEIGHBOR

Just remember that the vowels in this word are in alphabetical order (*e, i, o*), and you'll remember to put the *e* before the *i*.

POTATOES

Inside this word, look for three shorter words in a row: *pot a toes*. Thinking about toes isn't very appetizing, but it sure is memorable!

RECOMMEND

Not sure how many **c**'s or **m**'s are in this word? Think: **you wear one coat and two mittens**. That's one **c** and two **m**'s.

RHYTHM

To spell this word, remember the first letter of each word in this sentence:

Rhythm Helps You To Have Movement.

ROOMMATE

If you have a roommate, then at least **two** people live in your place. Remember to use **two m**'s when spelling this word.

SCISSORS

You use a **pair** of scissors, so put a **pair** of **S**'s in the middle of this word. You'll also need one in the beginning and another at the end.

SKIING

When you go skiing, you need two poles, so think of those and put two *i*'s in the middle of this word.

THOROUGH

Since a tho<u>rough</u> examination can be rough, make sure you spell the end of the word *r–o–u–g–h*.

TOGETHER

Inside this word, look for three shorter words in a row.

Do you see "**to get her**" in *together*?

VEGETABLE

The middle part of this word is the trickiest. Remember "**get a**" as in "get a vegetable," and the toughest part will be solved.

I'M GOING TO GET A VEGETABLE INSTEAD!

WEDNESDAY

When I learned to spell this, I thought of the third day of the school week. In my mind, I made a three-syllable word–*Wed-nes-day*–so that I'd spell it correctly.

FUN HOUSE

WEIRD

Remember the phrase **"we look weird,"** and you'll know the first two letters are *w-e*, not *w-i*.

WE LOOK WEIRD!

A LOT, ALL RIGHT, AND NO ONE

If you're wondering when you should use any of the above as one word, here's a little tip: **never**. They're always two words. To help you remember, sing this song to the tune of "If You're Happy and You Know It."

A lot, all right, and no one are two words.
Yes, a lot, all right, and no one are two words.
Now there is no need to doubt it,
but you really ought to shout it, 'cause
a lot, all right, and no one are two words!

FEWER AND LESS

If you're talking about something countable, such as ice cubes, say *fewer*.
If you're talking about something that's not countable, such as water, say *less*.

For example:

I'd like less water and fewer ice cubes.

Water isn't countable, so you say "less," and ice cubes are countable, so you say "fewer." Which leads me to . . .

Grammar would be less challenging if there were fewer rules.

SAY WHAT?

A PRIMER ON HOMOPHONES

HOMOPHONES are tricky. These are words that are pronounced the same but have different spellings and different meanings. The next few pages have tips for ways to make sure you don't mix up your homophones.

BARE AND BEAR

To remember the difference between these two words, tell yourself: you use a **bar of soap** on your **bare skin**. And a **bear** can be a real **beast**.

CAPITAL AND CAPITOL

The word ending in **-tol** refers only to buildings. When the word ***capitol*** has a capital **C** at the beginning, the word refers to the building in Washington, D.C., where the U.S. Congress meets. I think of the word *tollbooth* to remember that the **-tol** ending belongs with a building.

You can also think of the Capitol Building, which has a great, round dome. An **o** is also round, so try to connect those two ideas.

If you're not talking about the building, you'll use the **-tal** ending. The word ***capital*** can mean money, a city that is the official home of a state's or country's government, or an uppercase letter, among other things.

ITS AND IT'S (A POEM)

This should help you keep from getting *its* and *it's* confused:

When **it's** a contraction, an apostrophe is used.

But when it shows possession, there's no apostrophe.

Grammar and **its** tricky rules are not too hard for me!

Its: Without the apostrophe, *its* is a possessive. Most possessives have apostrophes—as in the phrase "Justin's baseball." When you're using a possessive pronoun, which takes the place of the noun, there is no apostrophe—as in "his baseball." The word *its* is a possessive pronoun—as in "*its* rawhide surface is smooth." In that example, *its* is taking the place of the noun, baseball.

It's: This is simple. The apostrophe in this word ALWAYS takes the place of a letter or letters. Use the apostrophe only when *it's* is short for *it is* or *it has*—as in "*it's* a fastball" or "*it's* always been my dream to pitch."

NEW, KNEW, AND GNU

These three words begin with different letters, but they sound identical.

New: This means having just come into being, fresh, or modern. Example: These are **new** textbooks.

Knew: The *k* at the beginning of this word might remind you of the words *knowledge* or *know*. **Knew** is the past tense of *know*, as in, "I **knew** I shouldn't have thrown that snowball at the principal."

Gnu: This animal is a furry, four-legged member of the African antelope family. If you know this fact, you know more than 90 percent of adults. Example: Did you see the **gnu** at the zoo?

Just for fun, let's use all three in a sentence:

I knew the gnu

was new in school.

THEIR, THERE, AND THEY'RE

These three are simple if you look closely at the spelling of each word.

Their: This refers almost exclusively to people. An *heir* is a person who inherits something, and you can see that word in the last four letters of *their*. Example: **Their** house was at the corner of Wexler Avenue and Lerner Drive.

There: This refers to a place and is easy to remember because it has the word *here* as the last four letters. Example: She has lived **there** for two years.

They're: This one, as you can see, has an apostrophe. It is a shortened version, or contraction, of the words *they are*. Example: **They're** painting their house with purple polka dots.

LERNER DR.　WEXLER AVE.

TWO, TOO, AND TO

Two: This begins with a *t-w*, so think of the related words *twenty* and *twice*, and you won't have any trouble. Example: There were *two* stacks of pancakes.

Too: This means also, as in "me, *too*!" It can refer to having more than is needed, as in "*too* many." Think of more, and it will remind you to add one more *o* to the word *to*. Example: I ate *too* many pancakes.

To: This is for any use that doesn't fit the two examples above, as in "All these pancakes and spelling rules are causing me *to* barf."

GLOSSARY

absence: when someone is not present (*see* p. 6)

arithmetic: the science of numbers and math, including the basic steps of addition, subtraction, multiplication, and division (*see* p. 7)

attendance: when someone is present (*see* p. 8)

background: the scenery behind something. The part of a picture that is behind the main subject is the background. (*see* p. 9)

balloon: a thin piece of rubber that is blown up like a ball and used as a decoration (*see* p. 10)

because: a connecting word that explains the reason for something (*see* p. 11)

believe: to feel sure that an idea or statement is true (*see* p. 12)

conscience: your sense of right and wrong that makes you feel guilty when you do something wrong (*see* p. 13)

contagious: a contagious disease can be spread by coming into contact with someone who already has it (*see* p. 14)

dessert: a sweet food that is usually served at the end of a meal (*see* p. 15)

February: the second month of the year, after January and before March (*see* p. 16)

friend: a person you know well and you enjoy being with (*see* p. 17)

height: a measurement of how high something is (*see* p. 18)

homophones: words that have the same pronunciation but different spellings and different meanings (*see* pp. 38-45)

instrument: an object that you use to make music (*see* p. 19)

juggle: to keep a set of balls, clubs, or other objects moving through the air by repeatedly throwing them up and catching them again (*see* p. 20)

license: a document or object giving permission for you to do something or own something (*see* p. 21)

misspell: to spell a word incorrectly (*see* p. 22)

mnemonic: a trick or device that helps you remember something (*see* pp. 4-5)

necessary: if something is necessary, you have to do or have it (*see* p. 23)

neighbor: a person who lives next door to you or near you (*see* p. 24)

potatoes: underground tubers (stems) of a plant that you can eat (*see* p. 25)

rawhide: the skin of a cow (*see* p. 41)

recommend: to suggest as good (*see* p. 26)

rhythm: a steady beat in music, poetry, or dance (*see* p. 27)

roommate: the person with whom you share a room or living space (*see* p. 28)

scissors: a sharp tool with two blades that cut through materials like paper or cloth (*see* p. 29)

skiing: a sport that involves gliding over snow on long, thin runners called skis (*see* p. 30)

thorough: careful and complete (*see* p. 31)

together: in the same place or at the same time (*see* p. 32)

vegetable: a plant grown as food. Vegetables are usually eaten as side dishes or in salads. (*see* p. 33)

Wednesday: the fourth day of the week, after Tuesday and before Thursday (*see* p. 34)

weird: strange or mysterious (*see* p. 35)

READ ON!

BOOKS

Cleary, Brian. *How Much Can a Bare Bear Bear?: What Are Homonyms and Homophones?* Minneapolis: Millbrook Press, 2005.

Terban, Marvin. *Eight Ate: A Feast of Homonym Riddles.* New York: Clarion Books, 1982.

Terban, Marvin. *The Scholastic Dictionary of Spelling.* New York: Scholastic Reference, 2006.

Trinkle, Barrie, Carolyn Andrews, and Paige Kimball. *How to Spell Like a Champ.* New York: Workman Pub., 2006.

WEBSITES

Funbrain.com Spelling
http://www.funbrain.com/spell/index.html
Find the misspelled word and provide the correct spelling in this game. You can choose an easy level or a hard level.

Quia-Homographs
http://www.quia.com/cb/96929.html
In this game, you read two definitions for a word and then guess what the word is.

Word Safari Game
http://www.netrover
.com/~kingskid/
Safari/safari.htm
Enter up to eight
words from your
spelling list and
practice spelling them
by playing this game.

INDEX